SCIENCE KIDS
The Changing Earth

HOW WIND SHAPES THE EARTH

By Megan Cuthbert and Katie Gillespie

LET'S READ

AV²

BY WEIGL™

ADDED VALUE • AUDIO VISUAL

Go to **www.av2books.com,** and enter this book's unique code.

BOOK CODE

G674831

AV² by Weigl brings you media enhanced books that support active learning.

AV² provides enriched content that supplements and complements this book. Weigl's AV² books strive to create inspired learning and engage young minds in a total learning experience.

Your AV² Media Enhanced books come alive with...

 Audio
Listen to sections of the book read aloud.

 Video
Watch informative video clips.

 Embedded Weblinks
Gain additional information for research.

 Try This!
Complete activities and hands-on experiments.

 Key Words
Study vocabulary, and complete a matching word activity.

 Quizzes
Test your knowledge.

 Slide Show
View images and captions, and prepare a presentation.

... and much, much more!

Published by AV² by Weigl
350 5th Avenue, 59th Floor   New York, NY   10118
Websites: www.av2books.com   www.weigl.com

Library of Congress Control Number: 2014942105

ISBN 978-1-4896-1922-8 (hardcover)
ISBN 978-1-4896-1923-5 (softcover)
ISBN 978-1-4896-1924-2 (single user eBook)
ISBN 978-1-4896-1925-9 (multi-user eBook)

Printed in the United States of America in North Mankato, Minnesota
1 2 3 4 5 6 7 8 9 0 18 17 16 15 14

062014
WEP030614

Every reasonable effort has been made to trace ownership and to obtain permission to reprint copyright material. The publishers would be pleased to have any errors or omissions brought to their attention so that they may be corrected in subsequent printings.

Weigl acknowledges Getty Images as the primary image supplier for this title.

Project Coordinator: Katie Gillespie
Designer: Mandy Christiansen

CONTENTS

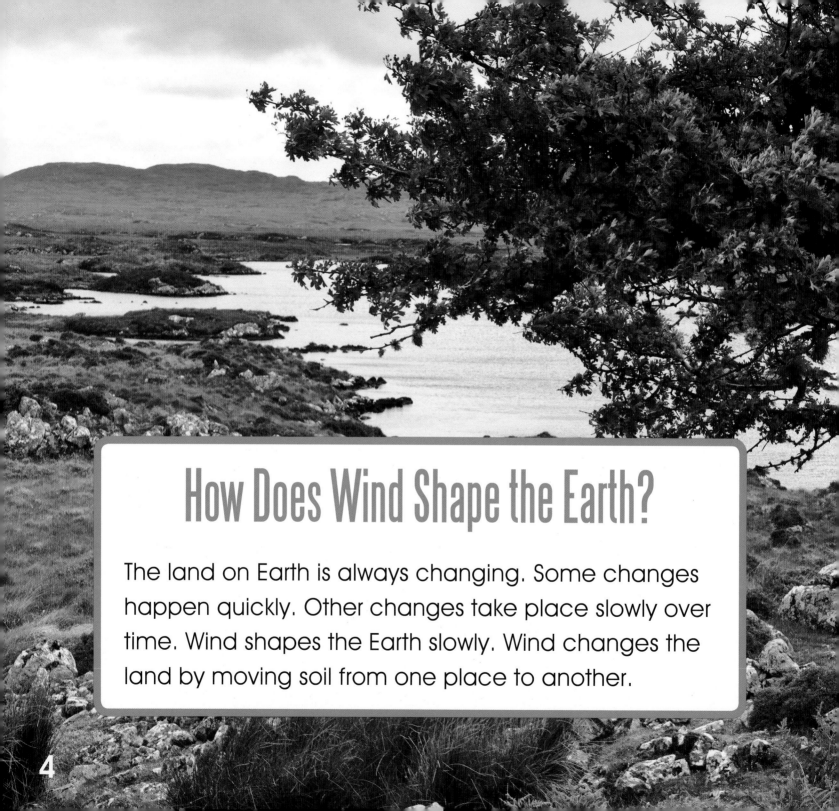

How Does Wind Shape the Earth?

The land on Earth is always changing. Some changes happen quickly. Other changes take place slowly over time. Wind shapes the Earth slowly. Wind changes the land by moving soil from one place to another.

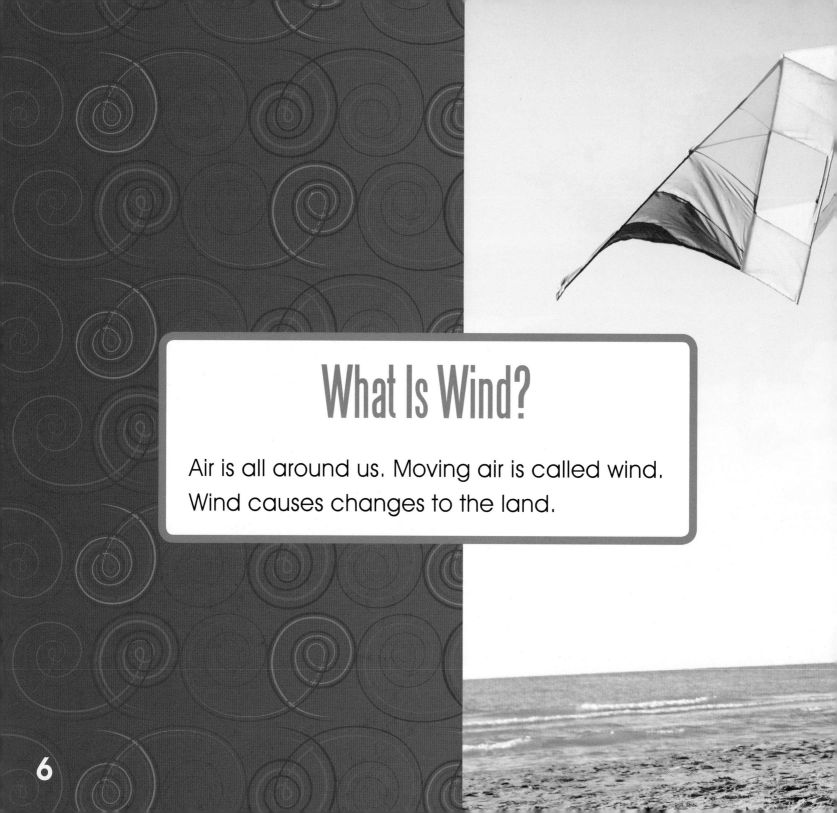

What Is Wind?

Air is all around us. Moving air is called wind. Wind causes changes to the land.

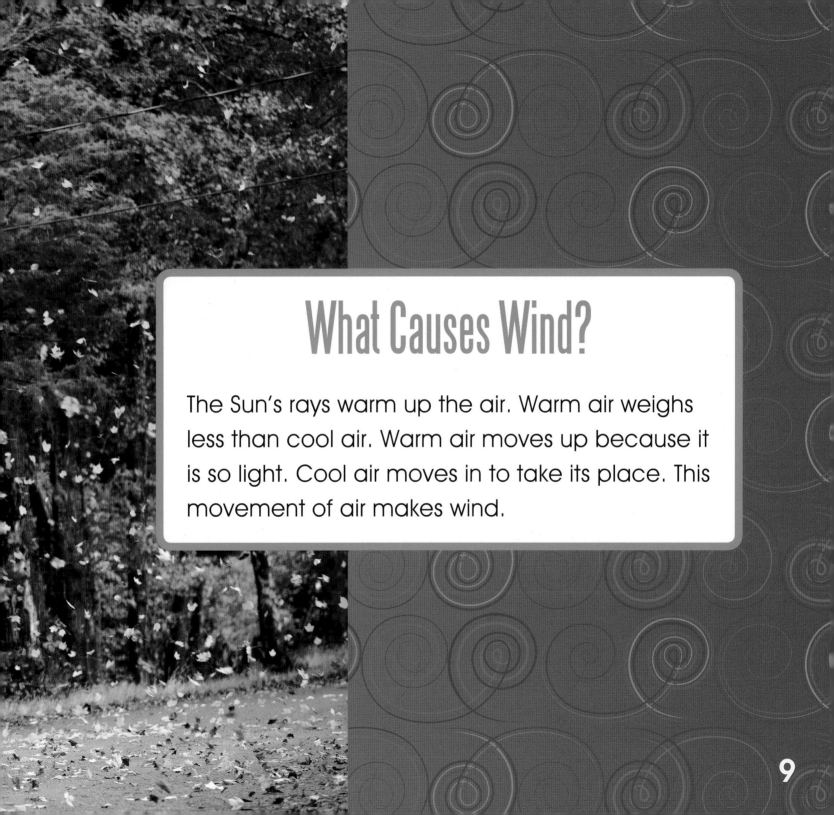

What Causes Wind?

The Sun's rays warm up the air. Warm air weighs less than cool air. Warm air moves up because it is so light. Cool air moves in to take its place. This movement of air makes wind.

Wind Is Part of Weather

Weather is made up of sunlight, snow, rain, temperature, and wind. Weather can be described by the direction of the wind. It can also be measured by the speed of wind.

How Does Wind Change the Land?

Wind can shape the land. It can make some parts of the land higher. Other areas are made flatter. Wind does this by moving soil and rock to different places.

Wind Can Be Gentle

Some winds are gentle. They blow at slow speeds. A gentle breeze may cause seeds to spread from one place to another.

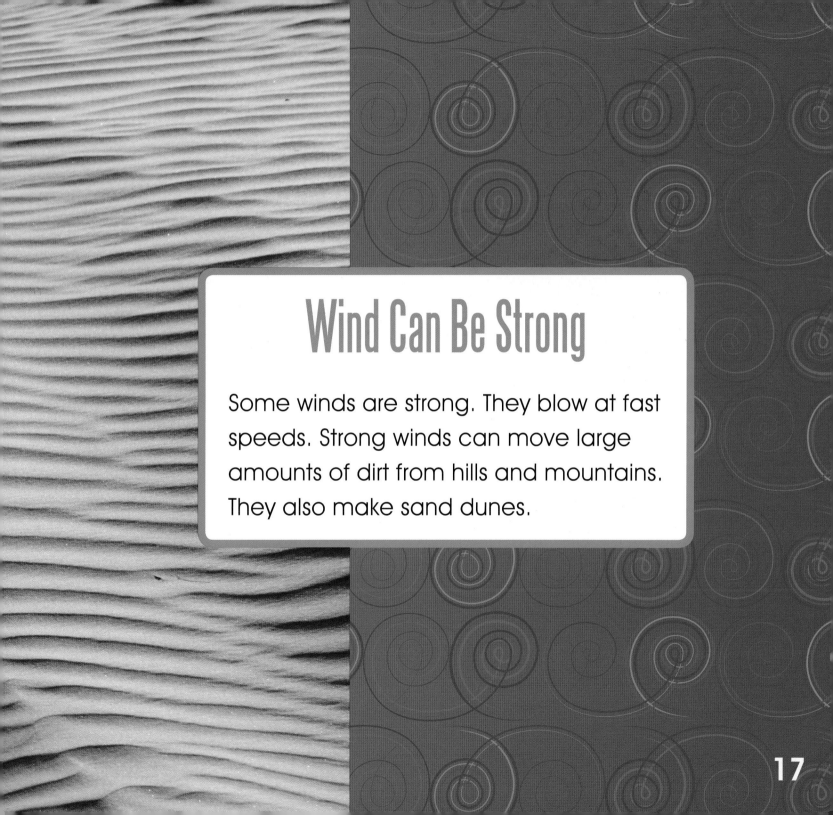

Wind Can Be Strong

Some winds are strong. They blow at fast speeds. Strong winds can move large amounts of dirt from hills and mountains. They also make sand dunes.

What Are Extreme Winds?

Winds that are strong enough to be dangerous for people are called extreme winds. These kinds of winds can cause damage to cars and buildings. Tornadoes are an example of extreme winds. The winds from a tornado are the strongest on Earth.

How Can People Affect Wind?

The roots of trees and plants hold dirt in place. People can plant trees to keep wind from blowing dirt away. People can also put wind to good use. Building wind turbines can help to power homes and other buildings.

WIND FACTS

These pages provide detailed information that expands on the interesting facts found in the book. These pages are intended to be used by adults to help young readers round out their knowledge of each of the natural forces featured in the *Science Kids: The Changing Earth* series.

Pages 4–5

How Does Wind Shape the Earth? The Earth's surface is constantly changing. Wind picks up soil and rock from the ground. It moves them to new places, which changes the shape of the landscape. Over time, wind can affect coastlines and mountains. It also creates sand dunes and changes the shape of rock formations.

Pages 6–7

What Is Wind? The air, water, and land are all connected with each other. Air that is always moving is called wind. It plays an important role in the natural environment. Wind can cause seeds to spread across the land. It also affects the physical features of the Earth. Extreme winds, such as tornados or hurricanes, can be harmful to people. However, wind power can also be used to help people.

Pages 8–9

What Causes Wind? The heat of the Sun's rays warms up the land, as well as the Earth's atmosphere. The atmosphere contains gases such as nitrogen and oxygen. These gases make up the air, which rises as it is warmed. Cool air rushes in to replace the rising warm air. The result of this air movement is called wind.

Pages 10–11

Wind Is Part of Weather Weather is the combination of different conditions in a region at a given time. Wind is one of these conditions. Wind direction is named for the direction from which it blows. For example, westerly winds blow from west to east. An instrument called an anemometer can be used to measure wind speed. The Beaufort scale can also measure wind speed. This scale ranges from 0-17 and measures calm to hurricane force winds.

How Does Wind Change the Land? Wind can change the shape of the land through a process called erosion. Erosion occurs when land wears away by a force, such as wind. There are two main types of wind erosion. When wind moves particles of sand, soil, or dust to new places, it is called deflation. Sometimes, these particles bounce and rub against the land as they move. This causes more particles to break off and get carried away by the wind. This kind of erosion is called abrasion.

Wind Can Be Gentle Winds that blow at slow speeds are called breezes. These winds range from 2 to 6 on the Beaufort scale. A wind that blows between 4 and 7 miles (6 and 11 kilometers) per hour is considered a light breeze. Winds reaching a level 6 on the Beaufort scale are considered strong breezes. They range between 24 and 30 miles (39 and 49 km) per hour. At this speed, large waves begin to form on the surface of the sea.

Wind Can Be Strong Winds that blow at fast speeds are called gales. These winds range from 7 to 10 on the Beaufort scale. A wind that blows between 31 and 38 miles (50 and 61 km) per hour is considered a moderate or near gale. Winds reaching a level 10 on the Beaufort scale are considered whole gales or storms. They range between 55 and 63 miles (89 and 102 km) per hour. At this speed, the surface of the sea becomes white with very high waves.

What Are Extreme Winds? Extreme winds can be very dangerous. These winds range from 11 to 17 on the Beaufort scale. A wind that blows between 64 and 71 miles (103 and 114 km) per hour is considered a storm or violent storm. Winds gusting 73 miles (117 km) per hour or higher are hurricane force winds. A tornado can produce winds close to 300 miles (480 km) per hour.

How Can People Affect Wind? By planting trees, shrubs, and other vegetation, people can help limit the effects of wind erosion. Farmers often plant trees around their fields to protect their crops. These trees are called windbreaks. People can also harness wind energy and use it to their advantage. Windmills and wind turbines are good examples of people using wind in positive ways.

KEY WORDS

Research has shown that as much as 65 percent of all written material published in English is made up of 300 words. These 300 words cannot be taught using pictures or learned by sounding them out. They must be recognized by sight. This book contains 69 common sight words to help young readers improve their reading fluency and comprehension. This book also teaches young readers several important content words, such as nouns. These words are paired with pictures to aid in learning and improve understanding.

Page	Sight Words First Appearance
4	always, another, by, changes, does, Earth, from, how, is, land, on, one, other, over, place, some, take, the, time, to
6	air, all, around, us, what
9	because, in, it, its, light, makes, moves, of, so, than, this, up
10	also, and, be, can, made, part
13	a, are, different
14	at, may, they
17	large, mountains
18	an, cars, enough, example, for, kinds, people, that, these
20	away, good, help, homes, keep, plants, put, trees, use

Page	Content Words First Appearance
4	soil, wind
9	movement, rays, Sun
10	direction, rain, snow, speed, sunlight, temperature, weather
13	areas, rock
14	breeze, seeds
17	amounts, dirt, hills, sand dunes
18	buildings, damage, extreme winds, tornadoes
20	roots, turbines

Check out www.av2books.com for activities, videos, audio clips, and more!

1 Go to www.av2books.com.

2 Enter book code. `G 6 7 4 8 3 1`

3 Fuel your imagination online!

www.av2books.com